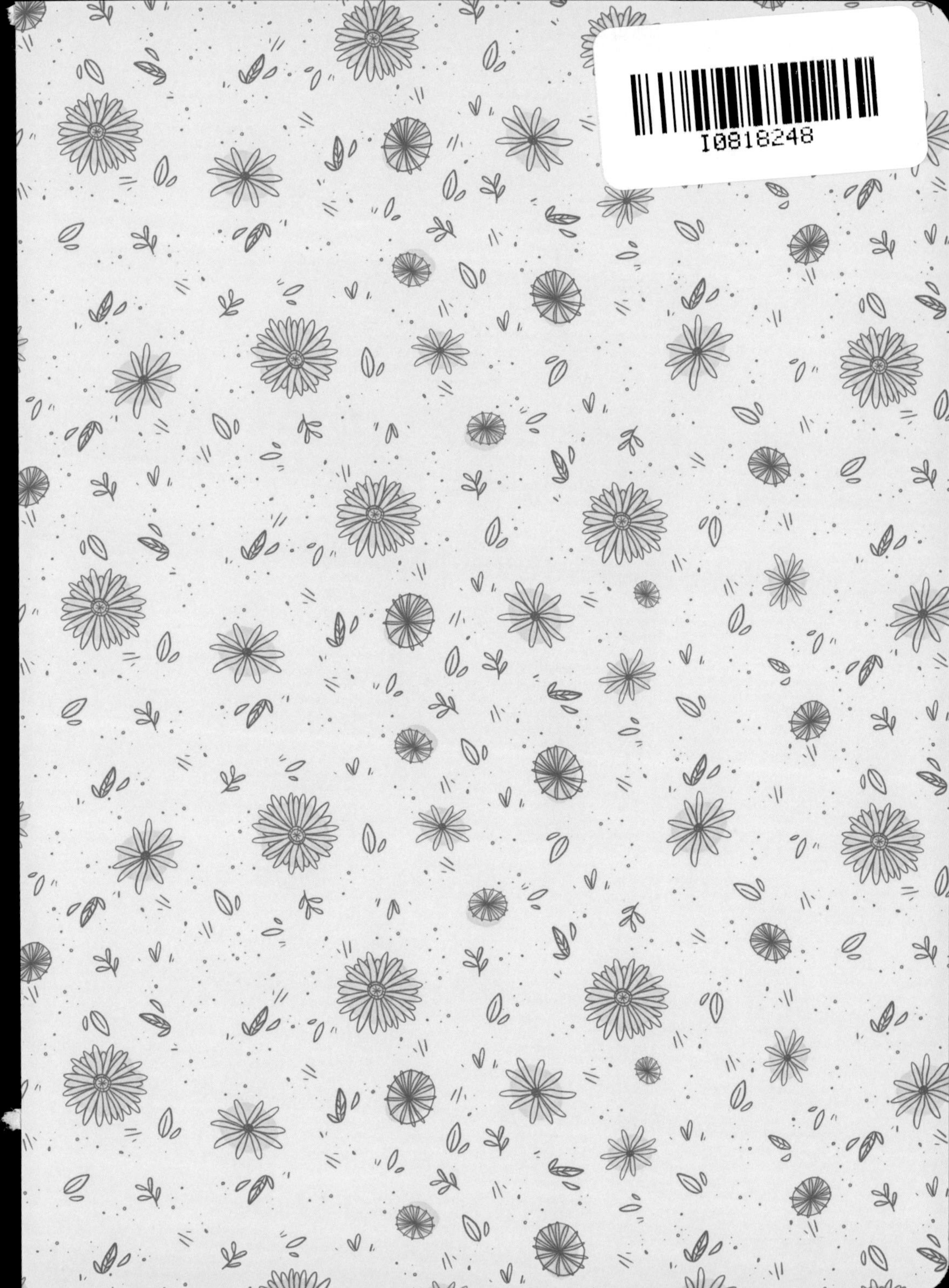

I0818248

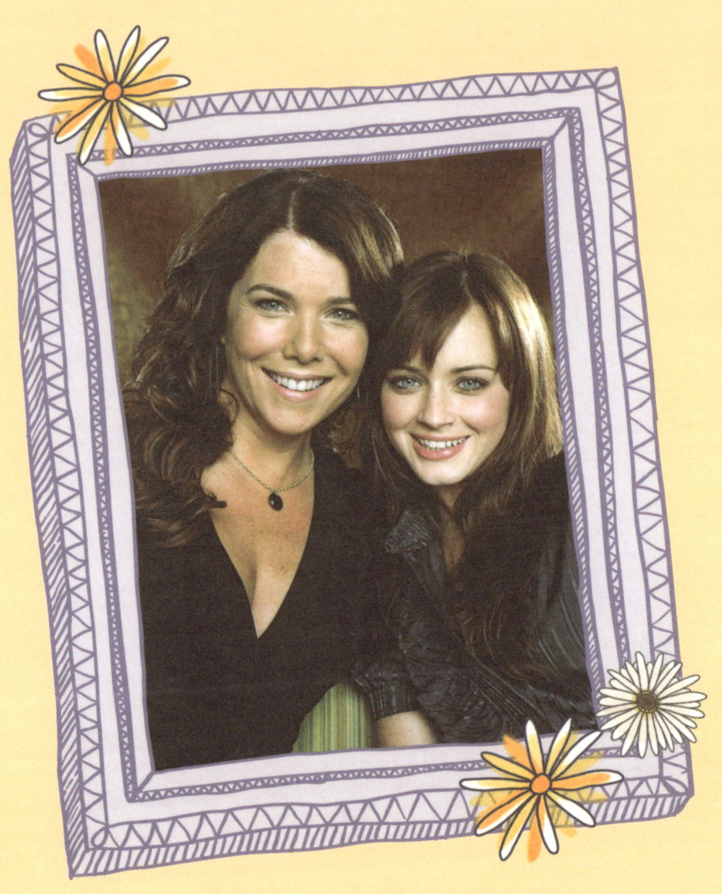

This Journal Belongs To:

____

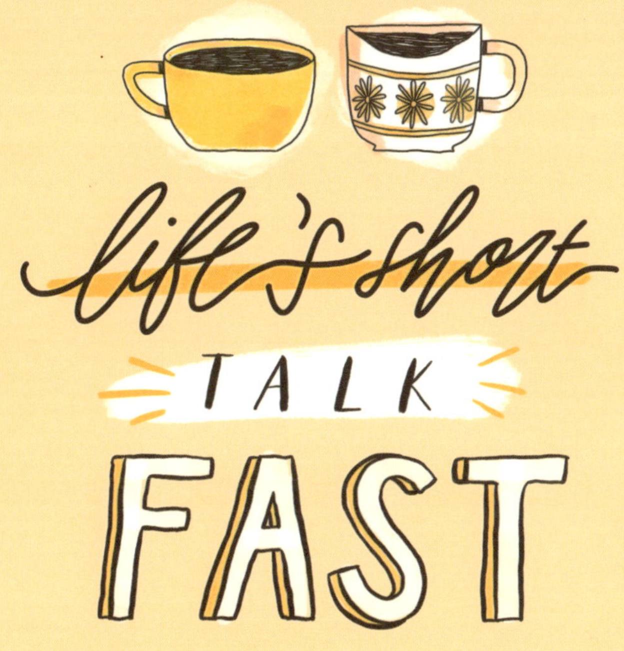

Gilmore girls

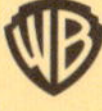

INSIGHTS
insighteditions.com

MANUFACTURED IN CHINA
10 9 8 7 6 5 4 3 2 1

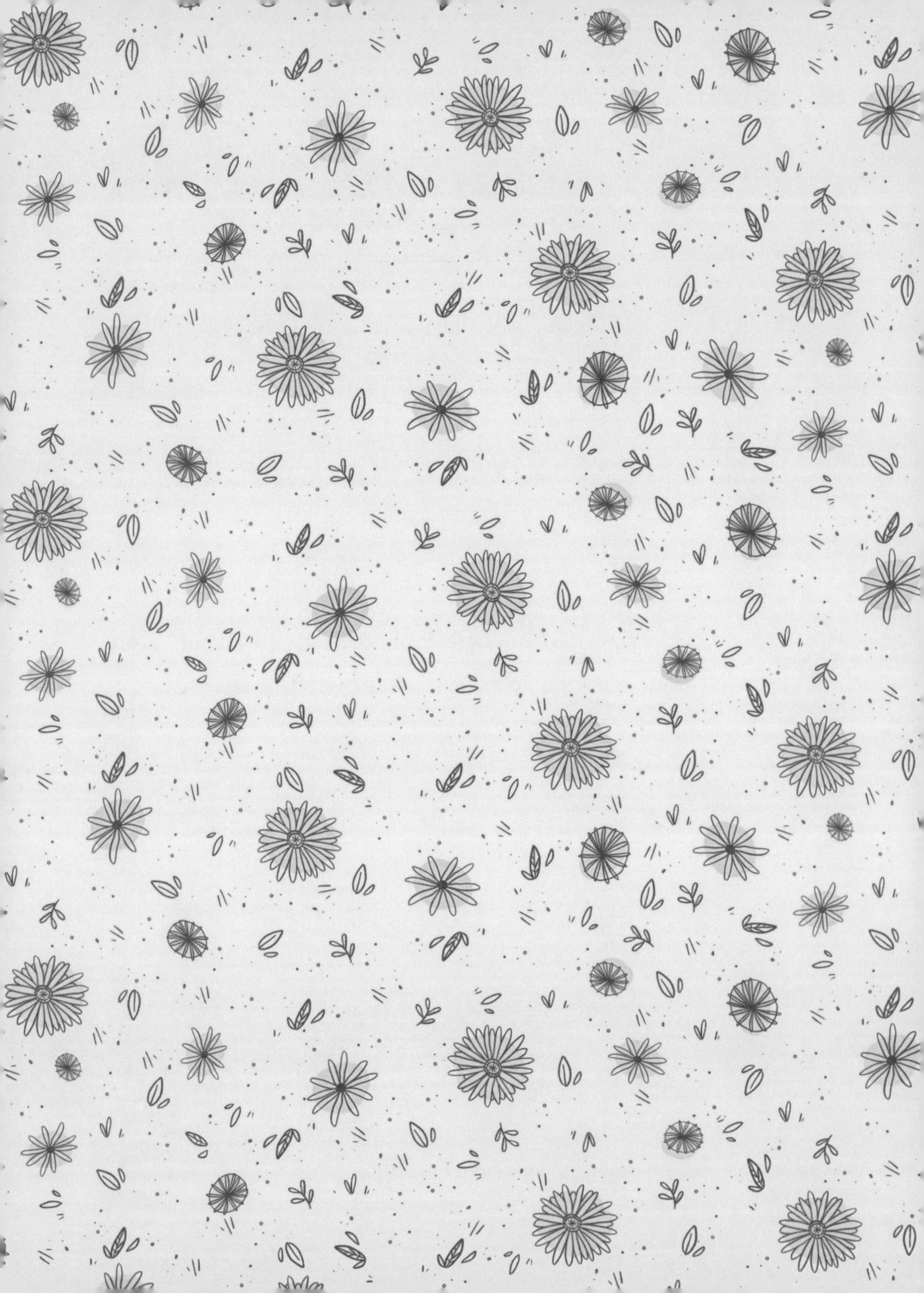